SECRET LIVES OF
SEASHELL DWELLERS

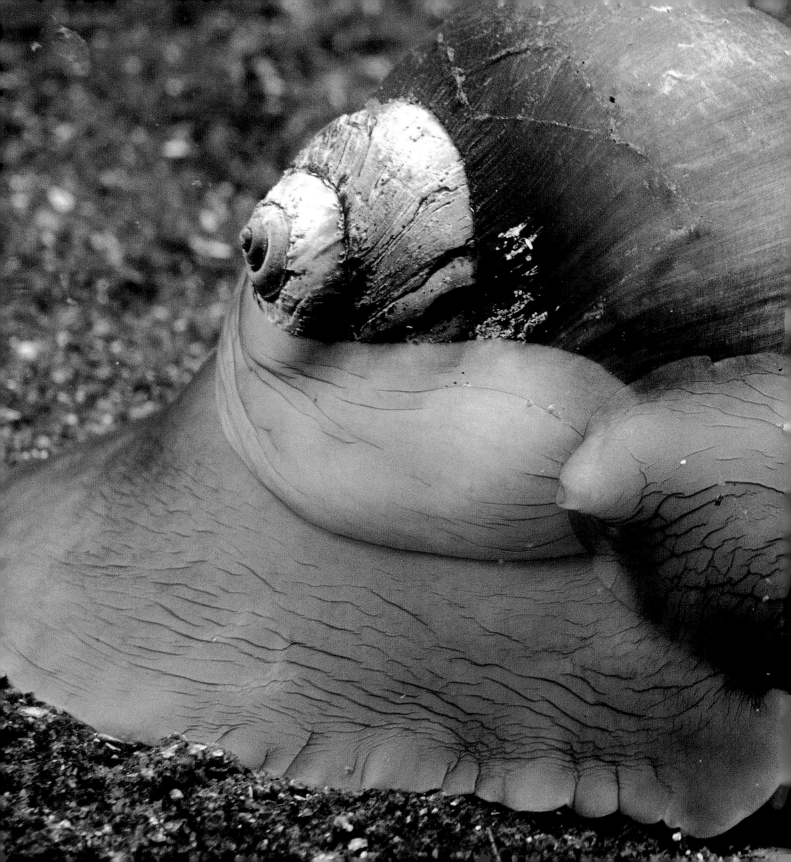

SECRET LIVES OF
SEASHELL DWELLERS

SARA SWAN MILLER

Marshall Cavendish
Benchmark
New York

The author and publisher would like to thank Sidney Horenstein, Geologist and Environmental Educator Emeritus, for his generous assistance in reading the manuscript.

EDITOR: JOYCE STANTON   PUBLISHER: MICHELLE BISSON
ART DIRECTOR: ANAHID HAMPARIAN   SERIES DESIGNER: KRISTEN BRANCH

Photo research by Laurie Platt Winfrey, Carousel Research
Cover: Alamy/ Premaphotos The photographs in this book are used by permission and through the courtesy of: *Alamy:* Tony Sweet/Rubberball, back cover; Premaphotos 16 + cover; Derrick Alderman, 23 top. *Animals/Animals:* Anthony Mercieca, 10; Ted Levin, 14; G.I. Bernard/ OSF, 22; Fred Whitehead, 31; Nancy Rotenberg, 36; Zigmund Leszczynski , 38; Color-Pic, 42. *Peter Arnold:* Gerald Nowak, 8; Wildlife, 21. *Corbis:* Louie Psihoyos/Science Faction, 32. *Getty Images:* Nigel Hicks, 33; George Lepp, 40 bottom. *Minden Pictures:* Scott Leslie, Titlepage + 23 bottom; Wil Meinderts, 12. *Photo Researchers:* Dr. Paul Zahl, 17; Andrew Martinez, 19, 20, 28, 35, 40 top. *Photoshot:* James Carmichael, Jr., halftitle; Anthony Bannister/NHPA, 34; David Chapman, 43. *Superstock:* Indexstock, 25. *Visuals Unlimited:* David Wrobel, 27.

Printed in Malaysia (T)
135642

Front cover: A periwinkle makes its way along a patch of sea lettuce, traveling at about 3 feet (1 meter) an hour.

Half-title page: This moon snail may look small, but it can grow its shell to more than 5 inches (13 centimeters) in diameter.

Title page: A moon snail uses its powerful foot to plow through the sand in search of prey.

Back cover: A sand dollar floats to shore.

CONTENTS

Every day, billions of seashells
wash up along the world's
beaches. Each one once held
a living creature.

BEACHCOMBING

DO YOU LIKE TO GO TO THE BEACH? What kinds of things do you like to do there? Maybe you like bobbing in the waves. Maybe you like building sand castles. Maybe you like lying in the sun with a good book. Or maybe you like walking along the edge of the water, looking for seashells.

As you walk along, you may see thousands and thousands of seashells. Have you ever wondered where they came from or what used to live inside them? The shells that you find on the beach were made by soft-bodied animals called **mollusks**.

When they were alive, the mollusks were well protected by their hard shells.

There are seven or eight different groups of mollusks, but the shells that you are most likely to find were made by either **gastropods** or **bivalves**. These are the most common kinds of mollusks. It's not hard to tell the difference between the two groups. Gastropods have a shell made of only one valve, or part, which is usually coiled. The name of their group, Gastropoda, comes from two Greek words meaning "stomach"

A nut brown cowrie crawls along the seafloor. This gastropod is known for its beautiful shiny shell.

and "foot." Gastropods seem to crawl on their bellies, but they actually use a large foot to get around. Gastropods are also known as univalves, which means "one shell" in Latin.

Bivalves are mollusks with shells that have two valves, or parts. The valves are connected

10

by a hinge, which looks like a row of small teeth. Bivalves usually keep their shells open when they are resting or eating. A broad band of elastic tissue acts like a prop to hold the two valves apart. When a bivalve is frightened, however, it uses its strong **adductor muscles** to shut itself tight.

The largest group of mollusks by far is the gastropods. In fact, three-fourths of the world's mollusks are gastropods. They have **tentacles**, eyes, and a single flat foot. A mollusk glides about on its foot as it searches for food. It uses its **radula**—an organ that looks like a tongue covered with rows of tiny teeth—to scrape off bits of algae and seaweed. Some mollusks even use their radulas like a file to drill into other mollusks. Moon snails, abalones, limpets, periwinkles, slipper shells, lightning whelks, and cowries are all gastropods.

There are a lot of bivalves in the world,

GASTROPODS ON LAND

Not all gastropods live in the water. Slugs and land snails are also gastropods. They lay down a trail of slime as they glide along, which makes moving on dry surfaces easier.

This mussel has settled down into the sand to feed.

too—as many as twenty thousand different **species**. They are the second-largest group of mollusks. All bivalves have a strong foot, but most of them don't move around much. Instead, they sit on the bottom or dig into the sand and wait for food to come to them. They feed on tiny organisms, which are filtered from the water by their gills. You can probably recognize a lot of bivalves. Clams, oysters, mussels, and scallops may be the ones you know best.

Gastropods and bivalves may look different, but they both create their shells in much the same way. They extract, or take out, minerals from the seawater. The most important of these minerals is calcium carbonate, a substance also found in many rocks. The minerals are carried through the mollusk's bloodstream to its **mantle**, which is a membrane, or thin layer of tissue, that covers the animal. Special glands in the mantle produce a liquid substance that forms the shell. Other glands in the mantle add a hardening material so that the liquid quickly becomes firm and strong. The mollusks form their shells in layers. Usually, the shells are made up of three layers: an outer layer, a middle layer, and an inner layer. Most mollusks add material to their shells throughout their lives. As long as the animal grows, its shell grows, too.

Every day, billions of empty seashells wash up on beaches around the world, and all of them once held a living animal. Think of all the billions of mollusks still living in the oceans and bays, where you don't see them. What are these mollusks like? Exactly how do they eat and breathe? How do they produce their young? What are their babies like? Let's explore the secret lives of seashell dwellers to find out!

Periwinkles like
to feed on soft,
slimy algae.

GASTROPODS

PERIWINKLES

PERIWINKLES GLIDE ALONG the rocks in shallow water, searching for seaweed and algae to eat. They wave their tentacles around as they travel along, looking for food with their little eyes. A periwinkle can't see very well, but it can tell light from shadow and see some shapes. It can also smell chemicals in the water, even though it doesn't have a nose.

When a periwinkle discovers a patch of sea lettuce, it sets right to work, scraping at the bright green leaves with its rough radula. The periwinkle feeds slowly and steadily, until it is finally full. Then it rests quietly as it digests its meal.

Periwinkles spend most of their time creeping along the rocky bottom in the intertidal zone—the area between the high-tide and low-tide points. Sea lettuce is their favorite food, but they also like another type of algae that is often called "green slime." A periwinkle usually crawls along on its strong foot at about 3 feet (1 meter) an hour.

Periwinkle shells come in many colors, from black to green to bright yellow.

Sometimes a periwinkle will find itself on the sandy bottom. It is hard to travel along the soft sand, because there are no rocks to hold on to. When the periwinkle is done eating what it finds in the sand, it will turn back and return to its rocky home.

LIMPETS

Like periwinkles, limpets graze on the shallow seafloor. All day long, a limpet clings

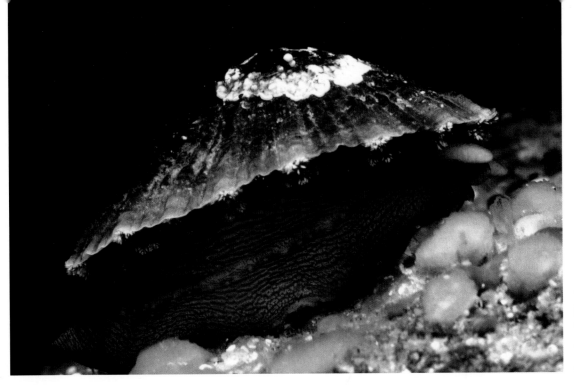

A limpet glides along the rocks, feeling for its dinner.

tightly to a rock under the water. When night begins to fall, it is ready to go off and feed. Rippling the muscles of its powerful foot, it begins to move slowly over the rocks. It looks like a pointy hat taking a walk! As the limpet glides along, it sticks out its tentacles, feeling for a good patch of seaweed to eat. It uses the tiny black eyespots at the base of its tentacles to watch out for sea stars and other predators. The limpet cannot see very well, but it can see the shadow of an enemy creeping near.

As the limpet leaves its home rock, it lays down a track of mucus. After a night of traveling about, it can follow its track all the way back home. While the limpet has poor eyesight, it has an excellent sense of smell. It can easily smell the chemicals in the mucus track that lead it home.

Some limpets always return to the same rock after a night of foraging. They fit perfectly into their rock home and cling tightly with their powerful muscles. Even in pounding surf, limpets can't be budged. A prowling predator would have a hard time prying one of these creatures off its rock.

SLIPPER SHELLS

Can you guess how slipper shells got their name? If you turn one over, you will see that it looks something like a bedroom slipper. While most gastropods' shells are coiled, the shell of the slipper shell is shaped like a dome.

Slipper shells also have another unusual characteristic. Most gastropods move about to feed, using their sharp radulas to scrape up bits of algae and other food. Slipper shells stay in one place and filter tiny bits of food from the water.

Slipper shells have a strange and remarkable life cycle. All of them begin their lives as males. Soon after one hatches, it attaches itself to something solid—a rock, another mollusk's shell, or even the back of a horseshoe crab. Sooner or later, another slipper shell attaches itself to the top of the first one. Amazingly, the one on the bottom turns itself into a female!

It's easy to see how the slipper shell got its name.

Before long, other male slipper shells attach themselves on top. There may be five or more stacked on top of one another. Each time a new slipper shell joins the stack, the ones below may begin to turn into females. If you ever saw a stack of slipper shells, you would know that the bottom one was a female, the top one was a male, and the middle ones were male, female, or somewhere in between. Because slipper shells can change their sex, there is pretty much always an equal number of males and females.

GASTROPODS

Most gastropods reproduce by releasing their sperm or eggs into the water, where the sperm fertilizes the eggs. But slipper shells do things differently. A female emits a chemical that attracts a male and lets him know that she is ready to mate. Then the male sends out a long tube and releases his sperm directly into the female.

Once a slipper shell joins a stack of other slipper shells, it rarely moves again.

Soon after the eggs hatch, the surviving young settle onto something solid and begin to form their shells. If a young slipper shell lands on a stack of other slipper shells, it may stay a male. But if it lands on a rock, it will soon find itself on the bottom of a stack of other slipper shells and turn into a female.

What happens if the female at the bottom of the stack dies? The next one up simply turns itself into a female!

SECRET LIVES OF SEASHELL DWELLERS

A female cowrie lays a cluster of small white eggs.

COWRIES

Unlike slipper shells, cowries are mostly solitary. A female cowrie will stay by herself when she lays her mass of eggs. Then she usually sits on the eggs, protecting them until they hatch.

After the eggs hatch, the tiny **larvae** float out. The ocean currents carry them far from their hatching site. In a few days, the larvae begin to grow their shells. Soon they also grow a hairlike fringe called **cilia**. Now they are known as **veligers**. The veligers swim about by beating their cilia. They feed on bits of algae floating in the water.

In a few more days, the veliger develops a foot, becoming a **pediveliger**. It drops to the seafloor and creeps about in search

Byssal threads, like these on a mussel, help some mollusks hold on to hard surfaces.

of a good spot to settle. When it finds a suitable hard surface, it attaches itself with small threads called **byssal threads**. Down on the seafloor, the young cowries finish growing their shells and turn into adults.

Cowries are favorites of shell collectors because of their beautiful glossy shells. Why do cowrie shells look so much shinier than other shells? Most mollusks grow their shells from the inside out, with the mantle between the creature and its shell. A cowrie grows its shell from the outside in, so the shiny mantle is on the outside, where we can see it.

Living cowries look very different from the shells that you find on the beach. The mantle covering the shell usually has frilly ornaments that help the cowries breathe and also provide **camouflage**. Many mantles are the same color as the seafloor or the sponges that the cowries feed on. It can be hard for a predator to spot a cowrie creeping along at night, feeding on sponges. It's even harder to spot one resting quietly during the day.

MOON SNAILS

Down on the seabed, a hungry moon snail plows through the sand with its big foot, searching for clams. When the moon snail finds a clam, it holds its victim firmly with its foot. It drills a neat round hole into the clam's shell with its sharp radula. In less than three minutes, the hole is all the way through the shell. Now the moon snail shoots digestive juices into the clam's body and shreds the clam's flesh with its radula. When the clam meat is soft and slurpable, the

Top: It takes only a few minutes for a moon snail to drill a hole into a clam.

Bottom: Moon snails have an amazing ability to take in water and expand their bodies. When fully expanded, a moon snail looks as if it could not possibly fit back into its shell.

moon snail sucks up its meal with its strawlike **proboscis**.

Sometimes a moon snail uses a slightly different method to feed. It takes in water to enlarge its foot. When the foot becomes really big, the moon snail wraps it around a clam and suffocates its prey. When the dead clam's shell opens, the moon snail can enjoy its meal.

No matter which feeding method the moon snail uses, it needs to get its big foot back into its shell after it eats. The snail solves the problem by shooting out water until the foot returns to its normal size.

LIGHTNING WHELKS

Like moon snails, lightning whelks are hungry predators. A lightning whelk on the prowl will bury itself partly in the sand and send out its long proboscis. The proboscis helps it to breathe and to smell. A lightning whelk can smell its prey from a long way off.

The lightning whelk's favorite food is clams. When it finds a clam, it pries open the shell with its large foot. Then it uses

the edge of its own shell like a wedge to hold the clamshell open while it feeds. The whelk sticks its toothed radula inside the shell to slice up the meat, then uses its proboscis to suck up its meal.

Lightning whelks have an interesting way of producing and protecting their young. When a mother whelk is ready to lay her eggs, she digs down into the sea bottom. She lays her eggs in long strings of disk-shaped capsules, which are buried in the safety of the sand. Each string may have as many as 145 capsules, and each capsule may contain from twenty to one hundred eggs. Most of the eggs won't ever

A lightning whelk and its string of egg capsules make an interesting beach find.

hatch, though, because the whelks that hatch first eat the eggs that share their capsule. The young that do survive—maybe only eight to thirteen in a capsule—make their way out of their protective coverings through a small hole and float away in the water.

ABALONES

Unlike moon snails and lightning whelks, abalones are largely vegetarian. They mostly like to feed in the nutrient-rich beds of kelp, or brown seaweed, that grow like forests in shallow ocean waters. An abalone will creep slowly through a grove of kelp, steadily feeding. It uses its strong radula to scrape up the kelp. All night long, it creeps and feeds, creeps and feeds. When morning comes, it clings tightly to a rock with its powerful foot. Now it holds completely still and rests. If the abalone is lucky, no predator will spot it camouflaged against the seaweed-covered rock.

When male and female abalones are ready to reproduce,

All night long the abalone creeps and feeds, creeps and feeds.

they release a tremendous number of sperm and eggs into the water. The large number increases the chances that many of the eggs will be fertilized. After the eggs hatch, the larvae swim about in the open water for a few days. Then they settle down to the safety of the bottom.

It takes nearly three years for an abalone to become mature. In her first breeding year, a female produces a few hundred thousand eggs. As she gets older, she produces more and more. When she is fully grown, she can produce an incredible number of eggs: as many as 10 to 15 million at a time!

Sea stars are just one of a clam's many predators.

BIVALVES

ATLANTIC SURF CLAMS

IT IS NOT EASY TO FIND an Atlantic surf clam. That's because this seashell dweller is always hiding! The clam uses its muscular foot to dig itself down into the sand. There it will be safe from hungry eels, sea stars, and whelks. When the clam is completely covered, it stretches its two **siphons** up through the sand. One siphon takes in water, which passes through the clam's gills and exits through the other siphon. This is how the clam filters water and gets both nourishment and oxygen. Its gills are covered with hairlike cilia. The gills trap food particles, and the cilia carry the food to the clam's mouth.

Atlantic surf clams spend most of their time buried in the wet sand, filtering food from the water. The clams mostly eat tiny organisms called **plankton**. It takes a long time for a clam to trap enough tiny bits to fill itself. When the tide goes out, the clam stays in its burrow, waiting for the tide to come back in. You may see small holes in the sand at low tide. If you dig down, you will discover the patient clams resting in their burrows, waiting for the return of the water—and their dinner!

In midsummer, when the water is warm, male and female clams release thousands of sperm and eggs into the water. The larvae that hatch from the fertilized eggs float in the water for about three weeks. Most of the larvae get eaten by all kinds of fish and other sea creatures. The survivors settle to the bottom and begin growing their shells.

A clam's shell grows from the hinge area outward, ring after ring, year after year. You have probably noticed the growth rings on a clamshell. Scientists can figure out how old a clam is by counting these rings.

OYSTERS

Like clams and most other mollusks, oysters start life as free-swimming larvae. Although mature oysters produce millions of eggs, only a few larvae survive. The survivors sink to the bottom and attach themselves to a hard surface. Sometimes they choose rocks, but mostly they attach themselves to other oysters in big oyster beds. Oyster farmers help create larger beds by throwing empty oyster shells back in the water, so

A huge oyster bed crowds a shoreline in Georgia, helping to keep the water clean.

PRETTY PEARLS

Oysters are not the only mollusks that can create pearls. In fact, most mollusks can. The giant clams of the South Pacific, for example, make beautiful black pearls that are prized the world over. But oyster pearls are the most desirable. They are treasured for their beautiful color and sheen, or luster.

that live oysters can attach themselves to the old shells.

Lodged in the oyster bed, oysters act like a filter, cleaning the water. They open their shells and filter food particles and bits of dirt from the water. Then they deposit their waste in pellets on the seafloor. Thanks to this natural cleaning process, other creatures, including sponges, sea squirts, crabs, and fish, can thrive in the clean water of an oyster bed.

You probably know that oysters can make pearls, but how? A pearl starts when a grain of sand or a parasite gets lodged in the narrow space between an oyster's mantle and its shell. Even though the particle is small, it is irritating. The mantle responds by producing layers of a shiny substance called mother-of-pearl all around the irritation. The mantle keeps adding layer after layer, until a beautiful pearl grows in the oyster.

MUSSELS

Like clams and oysters, mussels do not move around much. Only at an early stage, when a mussel has just grown its foot, will it move about. The pediveliger will creep slowly around on top of a colony of adult mussels, searching for a place to settle. With its sensitive foot, it feels its way along until it finds just the right spot among the other mussels. Then it anchors itself firmly in place with its byssal threads. There it will stay for the rest of its life.

Mussels stay anchored in place all their lives.

Using its two siphons, a big mussel may filter as much as 10 gallons (38 liters) of water a day.

Mussels usually live together in large beds, all attached by their byssal threads. Young mussels keep piling on top of the other mussels, until there may be as many as six layers in a bed. Being at the bottom of the bed is hard on a mussel. Silt and droppings from the mussels on top can actually suffocate the unfortunate ones on the bottom.

Like clams, mussels are filter feeders. They have two siphons. They suck in water with one siphon, filter out tiny bits of food, then send the water streaming out through the other siphon.

Female mussels produce a huge number of eggs. A large female may produce as many as 40 million eggs a year! But few of the little larvae survive to adulthood, because they have so many predators.

SCALLOPS

Scallops spend their lives on the seafloor. While most scallops can move about when necessary, they usually rest on the sea bottom, eating the sea grass. If a scallop senses a predator creeping near, it starts clapping its two valves together, releasing jets of water, and quickly shoots away.

With their little blue eyes, scallops can see better than other bivalves.

Scallops are the only bivalves with eyes. They have a series of little blue eyes, located around the edge of their mantle. These eyes are very simple. A scallop can sense changes in light and motion, but it cannot see shapes or colors. Still, that's more than a clam or an oyster can do.

Instead of a shell, a sea star has a lot of hard, sharp spines on its body. It is also covered with special cells that help it sense its prey.

MORE  FINDS

AS YOU WANDER ALONG THE BEACH, you may find the remains of some sea creatures without shells. Instead of shells, these creatures have developed other ways to protect their bodies. Sea stars have sharp spines that make them a painful meal for predators. Sand dollars wear their hard skeletons on the outside of their bodies. And some fish protect their eggs with hard cases called mermaid's purses, which are often found along the shore.

It won't take very long for this sea star to pull open the clam and devour the meat.

SEA STARS

On the ocean bottom, hungry sea stars climb over the rocks, sand, and mud, hunting for their dinner. If a sea star smells a tasty clam, it will creep over to its victim. Slowly it engulfs its prey and begins to pull the clam's shell apart. The clam's muscles are strong, but the sea star keeps on pulling. Finally, after about twenty minutes, the clam gets tired and its shell begins to open.

Quickly the sea star turns its stomach inside out and drops it inside the clam. The stomach begins to digest the clam's flesh. Hours go by while the sea star feeds. Finally, it digests the last bit of flesh and moves on, ready for another meal.

What does a sea star think about while it is feeding? Not much. It doesn't have a brain! A sea star doesn't even have a head. But it does have a very good sense of

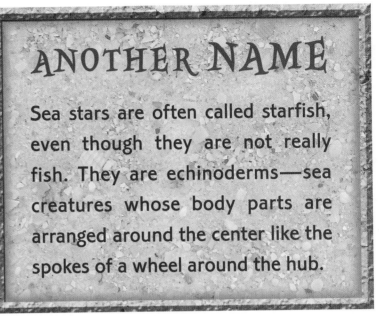

ANOTHER NAME

Sea stars are often called starfish, even though they are not really fish. They are echinoderms—sea creatures whose body parts are arranged around the center like the spokes of a wheel around the hub.

smell. Its body is covered with sensory cells that can detect chemicals in the water that guide it to its prey. Rows of sharp, bony spines on its arms and soft underside help protect it from most predators. The sea star also has very simple eye-spots on the tip of each arm. These eyespots can't see much—just light and dark.

SAND DOLLARS

Have you ever found a sand dollar washed up on the beach? It looks like a large white coin. It is actually the dried skeleton

Top: With its soft spines, a living sand dollar looks like a fuzzy cookie.
Bottom: Every hole and slot in the sand dollar's pretty skeleton once helped the animal live and breathe.

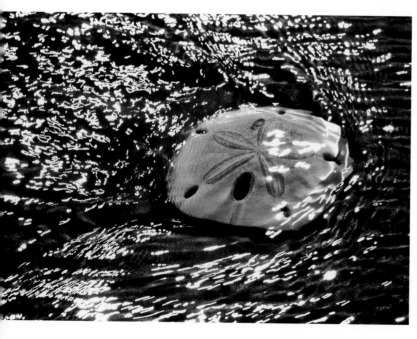

of an animal that is closely related to sea stars and sea urchins.

A living sand dollar has an external skeleton that is covered with tiny, soft spines, which make it look like a fuzzy cookie. It uses its spines to dig itself partly under the shallow, sandy sea bottom. It leaves only one small edge of itself poking out. Burying itself in the sand helps protect the sand dollar from its many enemies, including sea stars, snails, and skates.

How does a sand dollar feed? It wiggles the tube feet on its underside to gather small bits of food from the water. On its

SECRET LIVES OF SEASHELL DWELLERS

top, there are more tube feet, which it uses to breathe.

A sand dollar's skeleton is called a **test**. If you look at a test, you may see several holes. The round hole in the center was the sand dollar's mouth opening. The slot-shaped holes along the rim helped anchor it to the sea bottom. When the sand dollar buried itself, sand particles filled the slots. That made the animal heavier, so that waves could not lift it from its burrow. The petal design on the top of the sand dollar is made from tiny holes in the skeleton, where the breathing tubes stuck out.

MERMAID'S PURSES

Mermaid's purses, sometimes called devil's purses, are often found washed up along the shore. It's unlikely that these beach finds ever belonged to a devil or mermaid! But they certainly do look a lot like purses. And in a way they are. A mermaid's purse is actually the egg case of a shark, ray, or skate.

You can see the yolk in this living mermaid's purse.

After a female skate mates, the fertilized eggs start growing in her body. A yolk develops inside each egg, feeding the embryo until it hatches. Just before the female lays her eggs, a soft case forms around them. The egg case hardens soon after the skate releases it into the water.

If you look at a mermaid's purse, you will see long curly threads on each corner. These tendrils catch on to seaweed and anchor the egg case in the current. At the base of each tendril is a small hole. Seawater flows through the holes and brings oxygen to the embryos developing inside.

This is how we usually see a mermaid's purse—long after the eggs have hatched.

We have had a chance to examine just a few of the many different kinds of seashell dwellers and other sea creatures that wash up on our beaches every day. The next time you go to the beach, you can think about how these beautiful and interesting animals once lived their secret lives in the sea.

Words to Know

adductor muscles The muscles that bivalves use to close their shells.

bivalve A type of mollusk with a hinged shell made of two valves, or parts.

byssal threads Thin threads that some mollusks use to anchor themselves to rocks and other hard surfaces.

camouflage To change the appearance of something in order to hide or trick.

cilia Tiny hairlike parts on an animal.

gastropod A type of mollusk that usually has a shell made of only one valve, or part.

larvae The young of many invertebrates (animals without backbones).

mantle The membrane, or thin layer of tissue, between a mollusk and its shell.

mollusks Animals without backbones that have a soft body, usually protected by a hard shell.

pediveliger A mollusk at an early stage of life, when it has developed a foot.

plankton Very small plants and animals that float in oceans, lakes, and rivers.

proboscis A mollusk's sucking tube.

radula A tonguelike organ covered with rows of little teeth, which some mollusks use to gather food.

siphon A tubelike part that some mollusks use to move water from the sea through their body.

SECRET LIVES OF SEASHELL DWELLERS

species A group of animals or plants that have many characteristics in common. Members of the same species can mate and bear offspring.

tentacles Long, thin body parts on an animal that are used to feel, grasp, smell, and move.

test The skeleton of a sand dollar and some other invertebrates (animals without backbones).

veliger A mollusk at an early stage of life, when it floats or swims freely in the water.

Learning More

BOOKS

Beckett-Bowman, Lucy. *Seashore*. London: Usborne Publishing, 2008.

Kinghorn, Jenna. *Seashore Life*. Washington, DC: National Geographic Society Children's Books, 2002.

Theodorou, Rod. *Along the Seashore*. Chicago: Heinemann Library, 2000.

Tibbitts, Christiane Kump. *Seashells, Crabs, and Sea Stars*. Minnetonka, MN: NorthWord, 1999.

VIDEOS

Amazing Animals: Seashore Animals. DK Vision and Partridge Films, 1997.

Eyewitness: Seashore. DK Vision and BBC Worldwide Americas, 1996.

INTERNET SITES

COA Kids

www.conchologistsofamerica.org/kids

> The Kid's Section of the Conchologists of America Website includes games, activities, and facts about shells.

Enchanted Learning: The Beach

www.enchantedlearning.com/themes/beach.shtml

> This Enchanted Learning site has printable books, worksheets, and coloring pages on seashell dwellers.

Seashell Identification Guide

www.seashells.org/seashells/sanibelseashellident.htm

> The picture guide at this site can help you identify seashells commonly found at the beach.

Index

Page numbers for illustrations are in boldface

About the Author

SARA SWAN MILLER has written more than sixty books for young people. She has enjoyed working with children all her life, first as a Montessori nursery-school teacher and later as an outdoor environmental educator at the Mohonk Preserve in New Paltz, New York. The best part of her work is helping kids appreciate the beauty of the natural world.